OTHER EXILES

Also by Edward Brathwaite

Four Plays for Primary Schools
Odale's Choice

The Folk Culture of the Slaves in Jamaica
The Development of Creole Society in Jamaica
Contradictory Omens

The Arrivants
   Rights of Passage
   Masks
   Islands

EDWARD BRATHWAITE

Other Exiles

LONDON
Oxford University Press
NEW YORK   TORONTO
1975

Oxford University Press, Ely House, London W. 1

GLASGOW NEW YORK TORONTO MELBOURNE WELLINGTON
CAPE TOWN IBADAN NAIROBI DAR ES SALAAM LUSAKA ADDIS ABABA
DELHI BOMBAY CALCUTTA MADRAS KARACHI LAHORE DACCA
KUALA LUMPUR SINGAPORE HONG KONG TOKYO

ISBN 0 19 211855 2

© *Oxford University Press* 1975

*All rights reserved. No part of this publication may be reproduced,
stored in a retrieval system, or transmitted, in any form or by any
means, electronic, mechanical, photocopying, recording or otherwise,
without the prior permission of Oxford University Press*

PRINTED IN GREAT BRITAIN BY
THE BOWERING PRESS LIMITED
PLYMOUTH

for
My Father

Frank Collymore and Henry Swanzy
godfathers

Lucille Gill and Edgar Mittelholzer
ancestors

Henry Forde and Erika Ritter
other exiles

CONTENTS

Ragged Point	1
Journeys	3
Arrival	6
The day the first snow fell	7
Lion	8
Letter for Marchen	10
Cat	11
Blues	12
Basie	
Klook	
Miles	
Trane	
So long, Charlie Parker	
Bass	
Moor	17
At the death of a young poet's wife	18
Clock	21
Heretic	23
Judas of Barcelona	25
Machiavelli's mother	28
The Doktor	31
Schooner	33
Dives	35
Journal	36
Conqueror	38
Labourer	42
Comfort	44
Builder	46
Dred	47
Citadel	49
New Year Letter	51

ACKNOWLEDGEMENTS

Several of the poems in this collection, or versions of them, have appeared in the following publications:

Bim, the BBC's *Caribbean Voices, Delta, Cambridge Writing, Pem, Caribbean Quarterly, Kyk-over-al, The Sunday Gleaner, The London Magazine, The Sunday Times, The Critical Quarterly, The New York Times, The Literary Half-Yearly, Okike, Now, Breaklight, New writing from the Caribbean*

Ragged Point

New year's morning and we searched
in vain for the dawn: cloud-
carpet over the sea, light
seeping through like a slow stain

we watched what there was to watch
saw the cold rocks come clearer
sky rise. and we knew then

that this would be the year
of the great failure: what
we had always expected, feared,
never really wanted

next morning the weather was clear
we'd forgotten our notions: blue
sky and a beach black with bathers,
pleasure boats, horns hooting, steamed into the harbours

we travelled

far-off places seemed nearer: the telephone,
letter, personal messages, kept us content
like ships near a harbour. no danger
lurked in the postman's nook,

in the envelopes opened and read

and then one innocent weekday
just before lunch, mind only on lunch
not on fear or on failure
I switched on the news and heard

you were dead

banged head against the walls
of a bank, burst brains out
chained in the mad house
soft in a sad cell

shot in the neck as you turned
to smile and the heart's beat-
en drum, dumb in the sun-
light forever

and this failure returns me now

to that new year's morning: the dawn
coming up, the sun silent light
on the rocks, on the edge
of our island and the sea

saying silence unshattered
by wounds and by bullets
but the fear of it there in the cold
and the dark wind

Journeys

1

He was born where the path runs up the hill with little
children who laugh and point to the sea
and older they discover that the brittle
sand it washes is possessed by millionaires

he knew he remembered old women
who sewed old clothes by the lamp
but he couldn't remember the woman
who went to sleep in the damp

only her chair
in the corner, by the wattle under the hill
which spilled its birds in sun-
light all over the window-sill

the sun is a scourge of white, my boy,
the black night longs for the noon
there's soil for you at the end of the well
but a cow jumps over the moon

2

he went to the wrong schools;
was friendly with black faces
like his own, but was told their tales

were wrong; saw those who taught
him songs of what he ought to, what he ought
not do, take off their hats to the white

inspector's car. learn your books good,
lookin
good like him. ponds beauty cream

will lighten the skin and the black night longs for the moon
an old cracked face looks up from the well
and the dish run away with the spoon

3

so he grew up and his old instincts died like flies;
was told he should not leap the saddle
but scratch dry books to find where his spring lay

and although he did not know it then,
the historians were fools
who taught him rousseau's dictum as a book affair

for behind the spectacles and speeches
behind the front rows at the speech-day plays
he watched the seas of noon-dragged aunts and mothers:
black galley slaves of prayer.

but all his thoughts were chained
which should have sparked and hammered in his brain
but that the teachers taught him not to think
of things not on curriculum

what's more
he learned that nearly all his friends
had come to be content with sub-committees
or with some bankrupt chapel in a parish of cracked bells;

that they believed a tie on sundays and a well-
brushed blazer, paved them a way to old-age heavens
paper-lined with pensions.
and older women went to funerals of girls

who died hot stretched and soft with fever
because they could not pay the doctor's fees
or were too proud to take the neighbour's gift of eggs.
and to the bleeding child's relations came the black bible'd com-
    forters:

the lord is love, he will provide
salvation army blankets
though they could hardly dare to think
that cynthia who spat her lungs up pink

at night, would find a place beside
the parson's pampered blue eye'd child.
there'd be imperial preference up above;
eternal colour prejudice and love

4

where are the friends who ran with sunlight in their eyes
bright and upright as grass

where are they now after the young imagination
had attracted lies?

we seek we seek
but find no one to speak

the words to save
us: search

there is no destination
our prayers reach

no sun

no common sum
no good beyond our gods

of righteousness and mammon

Arrival

His first feet arrived and stumbled over stones
took the wrong turnings, lost

then came his guts, flexing
his feet, feeding him confidence and appetite, stealing

first pleasures and delight.
later he found his is-

lands: stuffed away in his pockets
the fingers tightly clenched

around a nervousness.
now the arms swung free

the fingers lost their nervousness
and began to ply their little tricks and trade

when the brain arrived, safe-
ly transported, telescoped and raped

he unpacked the wired apparatus of his eyes
so that he could assess not only surfaces

but doubts and coils: unreeled perspectives
could distinguish lies from solid ground

and his recorded mentums oiled like wheels.
soon he would play his part

all he awaited was his heart

The Day the First Snow Fell

The day the first snow fell I floated to my birth
of feathers falling by my window; touched earth
and melted, touched again and left a little touch of light
and everywhere we touched till earth was white

            wood was now black or white
            white world was bright at night
            and water was black wood
            carved into two white swans

            birth was black water
            where the white swans bend
            death was black water
            where the white wood ends

the day the first snow fell I floated to my death
of feathers falling by my window; left
love and melted, loved again to touch the little left of light
but all the world was dark while earth was white

Lion

When she arrives, sweet with devices,
I shall assert my courtship
tacit conquistadore with appropriate eyes,
ready to attest my chivalry with any cocky shoulder;
feel her elect my arm
stepping to town on her precarious primness

I shall attend her in the queue
smiling full sail into her windy gossip,
searching for golden spiders while
she spins details of some domestic cinderella;
sprawl guardian beside her
watching the lions blink and roar their royal unreality
wait for the screen to man its huge seduction

later I'll take her coat
observe the grace that turns her head like antelope to whisper
wriggle her shoulders
slip out her arms' fresh barley loaves
order hot soup
slit up her eyes when steam makes whiskers
coax me to half of it

and she will take the last bus home
turning a tarantella in her croton skirt
slip me her tip-toe dancer's hand
before she runs for it

like it?

sometimes the will that builds me up could break down laughing;
    no fires
flash their warm illusions in my room; at best
it's like those piccadilly nights; a facade
of tremendous lights rigged up on quivering heights

and I had hoped for power like that metro-goldwyn lion
or that I could command her wonder with some rumbling underground

Letter for Marchen

Sitting on the floor
warm in the coils and cinders of your hair
we shared, with our spared loves,
our fingers' didymus

for think, had we been born ten years
before this kiss
I might have seen your hair in conflagrations
your griefs combed clear as constellations

such little luck has given us this hour
such pitch and toss of time
that though our pilot lips
still find new trade-wind ways

to chart our universe
we are, at each completed circumnavigation
back to the windless wharves, the love-
less quays where hull the near-miss twisted ships
under the blind unblinking hiss

Cat

To plan plan to create to have
whiskers cool carat silver ready and curved
bristling

to plan plan to create to have
eyes green doors that dilate greenest
pouncers

to be ready rubber ball ready
feet bouncers cool fluid in
tension

to be steady steady claws all
attention to wait wait and create
pouncing

to be a cat eeling through alleys
slipping through windows of odours
to feel swiftness slowly

to halt at the gate hearing
unlocking whispers paper feet wrapping
potatoes and papers

to hear nicely mice spider feet
scratching great horny nails
catching a fire flies wire legs etch-

ing yet stretching beyond this arch
untriumphant lazily rubb-
ing the soft fur of home

Blues

1 BASIE

Hunched, hump-backed, gigantic,
the pianist presides above the
rumpus. his fingers clutch the

chords, dissonance and discord vie
and vamp across the key-
board; his big feet beat

the beat until the whole joint
rocks. it is not romantic:
but a subtle fingering exudes a sweet exotic

fragrance, now and then: you'll
recognize the odour if you listen well.
this flower blooms and blossoms till

brash boogie-woogie hordes come
bourgeoning up from hell,
blind and gigantic

2 KLOOK

The drummer is thin and has been
a failure at every trade but this

but here he is the king of the
cats: it is he who kills them

sick, sad and subtle,
from his throne of skin and symbol

he controls the jumping rumble
 using simple shock and cymbal

his quick sticks clip and tap, tattoo
a trick or two that leaves you

prancing: and reveals that perfect quattrocento
patterning: giotto, ghirlandaio, chano pozo, klook . . .

3   MILES

He grows dizzy
with altitude
the sun blares
he hears
only the brass
of his own mood.
if he could fly
he would be
an eagle.
he would see
how the land lies
softly in contours
how the fields lie
striped, how the houses
fit into the valleys.
he would see cloud lying
on water, moving
like the hulls of great ships
over the land.
but he is only
a cock.
he sees
nothing
cares
nothing.
he reaches to the sky
with his eyes closed
his neck
bulging.
imagination

topples through the sunlight like a shining stone

4   TRANE

Propped against the crowded bar
he pours into the curved and silver horn
his old unhappy longing for a home

the dancers twist and turn
he leans and wishes he could burn
his memories to ashes like some old notorious emperor

of rome. but no stars blazed across the sky when he was born
no wise men found his hovel; this crowded bar
where dancers twist and turn,

holds all the fame and recognition he will ever earn
on earth or heaven. he leans against the bar
and pours his old unhappy longing in the saxophone

5   SO LONG, CHARLIE PARKER

The night before he died
the bird walked on and played

his heart out: notes fell
like figure-forming pebbles

in a pond. he
was angry: and we

knew he wept to know his time had come
so soon. so little had been done

so little time to do it in

he wished to hold the night from burning
all time long. but time

is short
and life
is short
and breath
is short

and so he
slowed and
slurred and
stopped. his
fingers fixed
upon a minor key:
then slipped

his bright eyes blazed and bulged against the death in him then
   knocking at the door

he watched:
as one will watch a great clock striking time from a great booming
   midnight bell:
the silence slowly throbbing in behind the dying bell

the night before he died
the bird walked on through fear through faith through frenzy that
   he tried
to hide but could not stop that bell

6   BASS

Bassey the bassist
loves his lady

hugs her to him
like a baby

plucks her
chucks her

makes her
boom

waltz or tango
bop or shango

watch them walk
or do the 'dango:

bassey and his lovely lady

bassey and his lovely lady
like the light and not the shady:

bit by boom
they build from duty

humming strings and throbbing
beauty:

beat by boom
they build this beauty:

bassey and his lovely lady

Moor

After his rough-shod smiling prints,
he came to paint othello, smouldering moor

he knew the god of rembrandt
and the zulus
would not countenance a prince
whose rage was hidden

so marshalling forbidden firebrands of colour
he blazed his canvas with a shovel
like, as he said
a goddam engine driver would

the result you know: the monumental negro
turning from his love with his red dagger, iago

the violence of posture cracked
now and broken at the knees
and crumbling down to darkness
all the deeper for the colours that were there before

note the bright swords and jewels afflicted with the dew

At the Death of a Young Poet's Wife

And it was fitting that he should have noticed first.
he who had seen so much in people
that he acted out their lives before his friends;
he with such warmth within him
that he lighted up the house when he came in.
it was fitting that an actor should have noticed first

the others moved about the room, around the table,
stood waiting by the fire, arranged things on the mantelpiece,
picked up a vase and put it back again;
a painter, a musician: helpless friends

you waited for the doctor; moved quickly to the door
and threw it open, hoping against all hope
to find him standing on the mat outside
to hear his footsteps on the stair, the hall door open, slam.
your listening stood lonely, opening far doors.
then you moved slowly to the window, leaned wishes out;
the street was empty, not a sight nor sound;
so softly drew the curtains, turning back
into the darkened room, a helpless poet

and he had seen already, he who was fitted to have seen
so much. appearing casually to cross the room, he knew it all along;
went still to look but could not act before his friends what he now
   saw.
so stood in silence: helpless actor:
lost of all comedy: learning a gesture from her that he had not
   known before

o could the painter paint this scene
he who could carry in his fingers' diligence
green, sky, the crowded walks and alleys
of his curiosity: child, flower-girl,

the smile, the market-scene, the carnival, the queen:
and with his brush and pencil restore them to forever life
could he command perspectives now?

he turned
he saw the actor in his attitude
he saw the girl
the endless silence stretching out between him
and her lines her curve her colour the three dimensions of her
   getting empty

and there they stood: player and painter placed
before this girl who was not raw material now
but artifact: lips lids leaves of her hair
all fallen in a fine perfection. only remained
for him who spun his silver web of counterpoint
from air, to catch her pitch and silence

a requiem, a mass that would rise up from darkness
like a single vase in its complexity of lutes and strings
a patient web of singing love that would connect the room
crisscross of fugue that would offset the coming dust,
a lonely violin, a heartbreak harp. but turning,
the musician only heard the splintering vase,
only the breaking web, the snapping strings,
and beyond, a silence that restored them all

and so when you turned back from window's hope
you found a finished room: three friends,
the daily labour of their loves performed, only your lover
lying there was like a sorrow you had hoped postponed.
you went to them, their standing fascinated you
you wanted words from them but found they could not speak
you turned to her, her stillness fascinated you
you wanted words from her but found she could not speak
you wanted words for words were life to you
words to assuage a silence that you could not understand
words to refashion futures like a healer's hand

words that would walk long down the dark steps of beyond her bed
calling the gone-away the light the open door
the path of words from darkness that might have brought her back

and there you stood, lost beyond metaphors in search.
song gesture colour act: one word
would too distract the faith that followed you and fall
and be consumed within the depthless silence of your death

Clock

1

At last   that night   the pounding
in his dark released a flower

electricity of nerve   a blue
serrated fire   the scent

blooming with tears of glass
rounded him   he

unfolded e-
rect   a wrecked

calyx   what disasters unhinged
from his growing   what

impinges of pain   he stood
still   still

unable to move   his roots
moored in water   mirrored

through mud   anchored him

2

until the clock
wound up

to tick
the time

wound-
ed the rocked

skill of the
cradle, tell-

ing what-
ever tale

was tocked.
it threw

rickets into the
blood: an eye

opened on the
moon

tides of darkness
flowered flowered forward

corp-
uscles clicked

from the three
corners of the room

3

when the eye   closed
the

clock

stopped   and the   rocks of his skull fell down

Heretic

The little speaker, with his red
spade beard, twinkled at us for an hour
or so on the various themes of the age
five feet tall, but jaunty and fat,
he was dwarfed by the tall dark tales that he said

he threw the silhouette of sigmund freud
across our apprehensiveness, made him
hunchbacked and sinister, unshaven,
with blue jowls; showed us his satchel
of smooth instruments: psychoanalysis and
sex: saw how he chopped his mother, murdered
the thick-lipped saints and turning with his humped
up, dromedary back, jumped from the shore in a cockle-shell boat,
hooting his horn on the long dark seas of subconscious self that he
 sailed

we were relieved this dangerous quack was gone
shaken, we settled back
our lecturer assuaged our hopes and soothed
our fears, sipping cold water from his glass. . . .

the glass of water where it stood,
shining against the books and stones
was towering and cool
we longed to climb this tower
and escape this heretic and all the shams he showed
to feel the blue ice on our effort as we climbed
rung after rung of our exertions to achieve the top,
would breeze away and leave us strength for further rungs and
 heights
'til laddering up into the smooth round running rim—
aquamarine and green like brightest alps—
we walked its purest apogee, surveyed
our scaled achievements, the tilted landscape way below and
 temperate. . . .

but suddenly the tower of our safety was the tower of a town
translucent tint of water turned to blood.
the table that it stood on heaved and cracked
the flat walls bulged and bent. the dust was deafening.
the classical renaissance ceiling of our lecture room,
before this, smooth and bland, was blotched like sour milk
before the roof ripped off and showed the sky
confused and coiled, a boiling bowels of entangled intestines and wires:
rockets and wreakage, meteors and panic-stricken planes,
sky larks of parachutes picked out by lights
and stiller than the stars, grey weather
from the spreading bombs, roses and wreaths,
clouds funerals and broken jarrs, and all hearts
howling from the mosque of death. . . .

he paused again to drink. and in the pause,
we picked our powers up; stacked stone on polder stone
back to the speckless sky; rolled
carpet-grass and lawns, orchards and walks;
cut stone again and carved
it, moon-marble hard and smooth to represent our memories and scars.
this time, it seemed, these things would hold. . . .

our speaker paused: the glass half drained, our fears half
dwindled, heights unclaimed, the vision still foundationless
and taking up his notes again, continued

Judas of Barcelona

He'd dedicated to the city
this horned and crawling church no other

architect, he said, would have the fervour
to attempt; and the committee

gazing short-sighted at the plans, had blessed the 'sacred mother'.
and twisting unicorn and spider patterns, he'd built this witty

fever up three hundred feet before he fell. his mother
burnt the plans. no probes, she said, should ever see

the pity of her son's last silly escapade; no other
eyes should boggle at that final pagan paragon he'd

dedicated to the city. the nervous warped façade soon slowly
fell. one little room remained intact: the crypt

beneath the silly
project, dedicated to the city, with softer

care than worms, he'd hollowed out a tiny
sacristy, lighted by yellow candles; and in a niche, this carver

of great giddying cathedral stones had cut a holy
image of the bleeding christ with agonizing thorns

and wounds as glorious as flamingo flowers. he
loved this holy image, only his brother

judas knew how much; who every
friday since his brother's death, shutters

and locks his bank, takes thirty shillings from the tally
tank; crosses the road, climbs up the hundred

dragon-haunted steps to the three empty
archways of the 'sacred mother's'

incomplete façade; steps through one of the
archways, not into

singing aisles and transepts; but into the
decaying, littered workyard. here, like a ruined widow,

every friday evening he would pause, borrowing the
desolation until he felt his body stripped and tattered

into rags. he'd fumble for a candle stupidly,
light it, descend into the crypt. there

with his yellow candle, he'd suddenly
delight the gloom and sorrow of his brother's

holy image; and in the slotted box placed near the cross by the
committee—'funds for the preservation of the greater

church'—he'd drop his silver
shillings in. the architect had loved this holy

image; only his watchful brother
knew how much; who irrevocable good friday

afternoons ago, had pushed the builder
from the scaffolding, so that he fell down the façade three

hundred feet to that quick cracking blow: his jealousy
had urged and had tormented his pride so. and now he was the city banker

his name familiar on the stock exchange; and when he
walked abroad he could afford to bloat and let his business prosper

but why did this small cancer gnaw at him, a prosperous betrayer
in his guts: in this damp crypt, on friday evenings only,

why did remorse find light to kneel and was itself aneled?
but here he thanked his brother,

clutched the good luck this chapel was complete,
and genuflecting anxiously before the sacred sufferer,

cupped his fat hands around the instep where the holy
nails had festered out into a glorious sore; and sinking his head
   lower

reached its serenest core. this was the thirteenth wonder
the people of the city would never know another

Machiavelli's Mother

La porta de l'assandria: so we rang the bell,
staring up the hot grey wall to the twisted
grills of the balcony, where no flowers fell,
no lion-haired young women laughing down,
no flat signora's voice within
asking why all the racket
coming herself to peep and pulling her daughters in.
there was a large clay pot on this balcony;
but broken: the last black gritty soil
 chunked to its shattered sides, no hope for flowers there.
we rang the bell again, looking to the balcony;
hoping to see some tall romantic woman, mistress
of the place, lean down to us, placing a hand
upon the balcony, the other
on the cool brown rift of breasts
she'd try to hide as she leaned down to us.
but looking up, we saw no door, no window
opening on the balcony: what entrance-out was there
was now walled up, and to the flaking sun
 the house presented stolidly, a monochrome of clay

then all at once the great street door was opening
on creaky hinges, turning from within: but no one
stood there in the crack it made: it
opened of its own accord, impelled by some infernal agency.
so stood in sunlight on the threshold for a little longer
before we entered in: and found
antonio machiavelli
pimp and sometime railway porter
standing in the hall;
who grinned, showing tobacco teeth and
bony gums
and took us up the dusty stairs
to meet his mother

this shy suspicious lady, renting rooms,
moving all day about the house in cold blue slippers,
tousled hair and tiny pink kimono,
leaving her door ajar so she could peep her lodgers out
and in; who muttered to herself and shook
her head so that the papers clinging to her curls became
undone, and she would catch at them and absently begin to roll them in
again, peering the while beyond her work-
ing fingers—as if she anxiously were seeking family diamonds,
some fine dynastic jewels that were lost,
was all day—sweeping the rooms
and pulling the sheets—trying to find her son,
antonio: our pimp and railway porter

antonio machiavelli
had not always been the hollow six-foot vulture
that we knew. this pin-point-eyed cadaver,
who frothed and slobbered while he talked, had once been
choir-boy and acolyte at the capella san lorenzo
slipping clean surplices across his glossy hair:
lean as a candle and as cool.
but time soon lit his little candle, by whose light,
he saw strange visions: himself a smiling cardinal,
robed in red velvet, lifting his glittering rings
in benediction over the kneeling kings and temporal
princes of the world, whom he aneled at shrine,
advised at council table. and sometimes,
with the incense from his censer travelling up
in blue amorphous trails past the spiked cross
and past the yellow dove, he knew himself
saint michael the archangel, cleaving a path of smoke
and wreakage through all the brothels of the town,
smashing the day of judgement in the lechers' cups,
yelling from house to house his sensual apocalyptic news

but his voice broke, and he awoke from sanctuary dreams
to find himself a porter at the local railway station
toting the tourists' bags for tips and working overtime

among the leaky barrels and the sharp-edged boxes on the sidings:
heaving and hefting, sweating and trolley-carting
all of his dreams away. at evening,
grew morose and thin, sucking his melancholia
like a plotting child stood in a sulky corner;
and in revenge, sharpened a dangerous whip of wit and tricks,
cracked it among his friends, flicked it in wicked tongues
among the publicans, and posed among off-duty
prostitutes as an unusual raconteur:
so one day lost his job, spitting a hot white spider
in the boss' face: got drunk: came home: and slapped his mother

and she, adhering still to her antonio,
the visionary boy, became preoccupied
and shy, sweeping the chapels of her hopes
to find the boy she lost. so greeted us,
still muttering to herself, and shook her poodle hair,
and turned aside, still searching, to her room.
and there, among the sewing and the bric-à-brac,
she kept a bamboo casket
and pulling her kimono tighter round her
this little lady tip-toed shyly by;
slid back the blue lid of the bamboo casket
with its bright picture of lake como,
and peering mildly in the rustling dark,
sniffed the warm straw; saw
little pink eyes turned to her; wink and blink out,
wink and blink out; saw the soft heads,
the minute wet inquisitive pink noses squinting at her;
turn and delve back, turn and delve back;
making small cosy noises . . .

and while her son grew vulture-eyed and vulgar, tall with disease
  and drink,
this broken lady preserved his cassock and his candles and his holy
  book.
and though the pain she tried to hide was more than she could bear,
she kept her white mice warm within the casket
and every time she peeped at them, this mother smiled

The Doktor

Exiled from politics, defeated in his wars,
his life a failure, deserted by his wife,
this timid doctor turned his learning to the wooded hills

and there he built a cabin for himself:
three rooms: a kitchen, bedroom and a reading room:
but later turned the bedroom over to his tools:

the hatchet and the saws, the hammers and the various planes
he'd come to love: for he had learned the hard way
how to handle them: how to fell trees, cut lumber,

chop blocks down to required size for firewood or
stools: and stumping fingers, lost his clumsiness.
now with his balanced hatchet, he could split a stump

with easy chunk, and with delighted timing
confound the toughest knot: and working,
he remembered how he'd worried over tiny blocks

the way a mongrel hounds a stringy ham:
exasperated strokes would often miss
the block. until one morning, early, with the mist

still milky, his fingers found their way along the secret:
his hands now held the hatchet with experienced ease;
and to his joy he heard the conquered wood

begin to crack and sing within itself like little ants of fire.
now in his well-won mastery, he could have chopped
a thousand blocks that day and fed them to his furnace

nerves until he glowed like satan.
but he refrained from such extravagance.
the pains of learning labour taught him patience

and his days were not again wound up like ticking
clocks: time had become four seasons, and for him
the mild november's polychromes were treasury enough

and so he lived, season to burning season:
the rainfall stars upon his roof at night,
the clink bell mornings walking through the grass, the neigh-

bourhood of noon and shadows glowing cold.
wrapped in the seasons
and living with the trees, he never knew or cared

that he was growing old. until one winter morning,
feeling strangely lonely, he went out early to the ringing door-
step; stood with his hatchet at the chopping

block, and gazing down the brick-black path-
way saw some-
one, not a stranger, coming up the hill

who was this lady walking to his cabin
who sent this smiling messenger, this
shining harbinger, this

blinding angel . . .

Schooner

A tossed night between us
high seas
and then in the morning
sails slack
rope flapping the rigging
your schooner came in

on the deck, buttressed
with mango boxes, chicken-
coops, rice: I saw you:
older than I would wish you
more tattered than my pride
could stand

you saw me
moving reluctant to the quay-
side, stiff as you knew me
too full of pride.
but you had travelled
braved the big wave
and the bilge-swishing stomach,
climbed the tall seas
to come to me

ship was too early
or was I too late?

walking still slowly
(too late or too early?)
saw you suddenly turn
ropes quickly cast off from the capstan
frilled sails were unfurled
water already between your hull and the harbour

too late too late
or too early?

running now
one last rope stretched
to the dockside
tripping over a chain—
chink in my armour—

but the white bows were turning
stern coming round squat in the water

and I
older now
more torn and tattered than my pride
could stand
stretch out my love to you across the water
but cannot reach your hand

Dives

Before they built the deep water harbour
sinking an island to do it
we used to row out in our boats

to the white liners, great ocean-going floats,
to dive for coins. Women with bracelets,
men with expensive tickers on their wrists,

watched us through bland sun glasses
so that their blue stares never blinked.
they tossed us pennies. the spinning flat
metallic bird would hit the water with a little

flap and wing zig-zagging down the water's track.
our underwater eyes would watch it like a cat
as it dark bottomed soundwards like a pendulum
winging from side to side, now black

now bright, now black, now bright,
catching the dying daylight down
the coal dark tides of the ship.
every shadow we saw was a possible shark

but we followed that flat dark light
even if the propellers would suddenly turn
burning the water to murderous cold
we would never come nearer to gold

Journal

When we were young we found life
flourishing: our mothers' love our fathers' confidence
our friends' companionships were rich
it was a bramble island life we knew
but still we loved it
preferring what we had at home
to what we'd heard about

when we went off on holiday we found love
was the only thing worth fighting for
the shining chivalry of walking out
of conquering new worlds for her
and home again we found the scope too short
our mother's worries too embarrassing
our father's bonhomie misplaced
our friends potential plotters seldom trusted

when we went off to work we found
that both had fooled us: life and love
the green life that we loved
must turn to sweat and stone
if we would gain the garden that we promised to our love
and sweat and stone was not the sort of life
we dreamed of where we lived

so we came on to paris new york london town
a little puzzled and alone
pretending that we scorned the little home
the earlier night-errantry of love
learning the odd trade here
the quite impossible profession there
and scattering a rootless crop of tricks
until the brightness of our hopes was sticks
and then instead of getting tough, became dog-eared and sentimental

took to forgetting dates, lay low in bed all day
talked of the days back home

so we returned pretending still we had outgrown the past
that it wasn't any use going down the beaches
or whistling as usual for the dog
it's only when we found that what we were pretending
was not there, was after all not there at all
that the horse and the dog were dead
that we discovered how expensively we'd fooled ourselves
we left home thinking it too green and hedged
mother's love and father's love constricted us
not knowing that our parents' love was mort-
gaged even before we left

and we went off from one who said that she would love for-
ever: believing she would wait and so give weight to our
desertion: but home again we find her house is shut
she went off with the one she loved even before we left

so here we are: stripped
sniffing like dogs from pillar to poles
running alone, lost, tail between legs
not daring to bark at the bone
since the waters' reflections are false
using the cracks in the fence as escape
holes: running from shadow to cold

Conqueror

1

From quiet shires of church bells, falling leaves,
to this salt turbulence
sand under my feet, pebbles, powdery hills

halting my innocence

from the wooden bridge, pub on the corner, its sign swinging,
willows in winter,
to this empty house, these windmills turning, turning

this midnight drummer

there was a king and his court, archbishops, churchmen,
I had nothing to do with them
I obeyed the laws, poured my soft head of ale in the evening,
   fished in all weathers

hauled my revenge of pale women

now I am king of the court, pay churchmen
to pull weeds from the pathway to heaven, send them
back home with the children as soon as the girls' pains grow red
   with the moon's change of weather

before the boys breed loyalties out of these strange women

at home there is a wooden bridge, pub on the corner, its sign
   swinging
willows in winter;
here there is this empty house, these windmills turning turning

this midnight drummer

2

like a rat
like a rat
like a rat-a-tap tappin

like a rat
like a rat
like a rat-a-tap tappin

we eyes we teet we eatin

like a rat
like a rat
like a rat-a-tap tappin

like a rat
like a rat
like a rat-a-tap tappin

an we burnin babylone

                haile selassie hallelu/ja
                haile selassie hallelu/ja
                haile selassie hallelu/ja

                an we burnin babylone

3

it was a victory for the chapels
blowing their bibles
black preachers speaking with the voices of conches

as toussaint did in haiti
as christophe died in haiti

speaking from the tongues of whips
tonelles

speaking from the lips of limp-
ing angels: loa

as the gods do in haiti
in liberated haiti

it was a victory for prayers
starched linen halleluja
pressed pants
barefoot respectability

drought no law no land
the pastors almost doubted

you ask for bread and they fling you a stone
no loaf no love no miracle

you ask for a roof: ceremony of the mounted dead
and your spiked head rots by the roadside

and then those eyes

      that could speak so sweetly
      burn so softly

      farms by the sea-
      side: green growing on green
      green glowing against the blue

      for now I would obliterate you
      from the obscurity of yourselves'
      uncertain silver
      from the feint hearts of your mind-

      less architects
      from the starless dampness of your leaking corners

      I would obliterate you
      from your self-cement of fist of rise of rocket

from the hatred of your dolour
from the inhabited dungles of no hope

I would take you into the home of the brick
the flat foot of the mortar
the spinning industrial space of the spider
the hounforts of favella vision

I would ask you to walk the four corners of your
    understanding
rum cocksblood spirit liberation

humbly to step from slave to certain owner
humbly to acknowledge mother father brother sister
humbly to break forth song psalm handclap petal
from the dungeons of unrighteousness

into light into stone into pathway into leaf
of hope
and the rope: whip tomb boulder:
that had bound you

now talisman now twisted into prayer now shredded into
timeless stars

like a rat
like a rat
like a rat-a-tap tappin

like a rat
like a rat
like a rat-a-tap tappin

an we burnin babylone . . .

Labourer

Look at his hands
cactus cracked, pricked,
worn smooth by the hoe
limestone soil's colour;
he has lost three fingers
of his left hand falling
asleep at the mill;
the black crushing grin
of the iron tooth'd ratchets
grinding the farley hill cane
have eaten him lame
and no one is to blame

the crunched bone was juicy
to the iron, there was no difference
between his knuckle joints
and ratoon shoots: the soil
receives the liquor with cool flutes;
three fingers are not even worth
a stick of cane; the blood
mix does not show, the star-
gaze crystal sugar shines
no brighter for the cripple blow

and nothing more to show
for thirty years' spine-
curving labour in clear
rain, glass-eyed, coming off the sea,
fattening up the mud
in the valleys, cours-
ing down hillsides, causing the toil of the deep
well-laid roots, gripping soil,
to come steadily loose, junction and joint
between shoot and its flower to be made nonsense of

and the shame, the shame, the shame-
lessness of it all, the name-
less days in the burnt cane-
fields without love; crack of its
loud trash, spinn-
ing ashes; wrack of salt odour that will
not free his throat; the cutlass fall-
ing, fall-
ing: sweat, grit
between fingers, chigga
hatching its sweet nest of pain in his toe,
and now this and now this

an old man, prickled
to sleep by the weather, his labour,
losing his hands . . .

Comfort

The little boys released
from foundry school
are unhappy with the world around them in the lower green

there is the noise of buses
and the memory of licks and failures

didn't know your tense today
your noon-day tables
didn't do your verbs today
didn't learn that word list
didn't earn those sparks
didn't clean othello's rusty swords

and there is rain in the desert
a whistle of dust
a dry leaf falling
bricks stones gravel

look me hey
nuts glassies sugar cakes cockies
who want me sweet comforts

and her tray is red
cool as angels
sugar sweet and freshly mined and minted

mother

but she screels at him
money money money money
not a penny less

the cracked nut-brown face
the black sour-sop eyes
the white headtie
the voice of the monkey

each cock she creates has to crow
its white peppermint of feathers
blue spurs red syrup of the glory comb
pale yellow beak of pain

it is her house at five o'clock
in the foreday morning
before the sun wakes engines up
it is her broken paling

dead wood yard
enamel pots with flinted patches
broken locks, slip-sided doors
the windows without slats

it is the coalpot where she warms her porridge
the battered saucepan where she boils her pap
it is the stripped and sheetless bed
the mattress wrestling with straw at her distress

her matchstick strikes a fire
sun/white
red/lantern glow
a creak of bird
a feather shred of wire
a crowing light
the listen engine cackle

and the bird rises from the rustle of her nightly yard
its spurs in the black earth
its plumage covering her house with glow
its stretched neck cruelling beyond her hard and cockroach
the red head crying from the shadows of her hair

nuts glassies comfort cockscomb

the boy reaches up towards the minted morning bugle
warming her pots she hears the rats teeth crow

Builder

Mr theophilis archer
    squinty cap
    long lanes of planes
    smooth runway facing the water

dreams of thin walls between his sons and the deep
sounding fish that his conscience will keep

but first there will be the resinous miles of red timber
wallaba balata hardwood
to be stripped of its scales, grey coppery bark
the bleeding christ of the amazon
succumbed onto rollers and rolled down the hill to his vision

spikes then, splitting the boatflesh
    and the sea breaking
    fresh breeze in the morning
    thunder of hoof in the green noons of august
    and the surf breathing rock
    and the beam leaping light over blocks
    and the naked ribs ready

then strip by strip
each fragile skin and tendon
the body built to slope and passage
nosing the waters
battering up in the tides
roving through smiles of the nibbling slanderous currents
the keel disappears in the shallows
like a fish slipping into the shadows of waterless walls of the forest
    and the vessel of breath he has patiently flared to a syllable

    floats   free of his now voiceless chisels

Dred

The law and its punitive measurements
   has been like a heavy hammering all these years
     nails into metal, metal into the unrelenting echo of the coffin

I have worn this mist and heat
   dead head of some blond barber's chair
   from fleet street, some voyeur from around the inns of court

I have become all voice and forehead, bland and fear
   even the window frames and frowns
   prevent my seeing

   fields, gardeners, the city's noisy caravels
   the dead bird fountain where lovers lie at night
   the soda fountain further down the light, where they first meet

I am allowed a woven fan of grass
   this shuddering electric monster, imitating wind in trees
   but no real breeze, no sky's blue story, cool of birds

this man before me now
   from dungeon wrack and police lock-up clammy jail
   his clothes all stale, his eyelids soiled

   from too much sleep
   too little food and fondness
   the black skin chalked for lack of rain

   rape me lud
   persistent robbery

I squint towards him
   woman? flesh? a subtle shaft perfume?
   a swimming fish in lighted glass he failed?
   his dead foot running in the long live grass?

a child perhaps? a son he loved? someone to fetch him smile?
a scrap of board he built sometime before the flood?
a window, selling books, calling for trust for trade exchange of
   eyes?

there is no echo back
   he looks bars through me, metal
   he sees: the clock, no sun
   the calendar is wasted years

   harbour rockstone bloodless marl
   and the mockingbird singing that he fraid karl
   my studdering electric razor:

   for what it is:
   a ban upon the mild november's breeze
   its memories of summer seas and booze

he hardly hears my dead wig's voice
   pause at the bar and falter

   son?

it almost says

   ten years

Citadel

At the pic of le cap where the citadel sits
the arawaks wait
the flèches of their headdress are bells up the montagne

the rings of the palm trees are bells up the montagne
toussaint is a zemi
he stares from the flesh of the stone

the white of the helmet, columbus conquistador
the white of the sword
becomes lightning

the steel of the cutlass
the knife of the god
thongs of the whips

drink water like trees
africaines from the slave ships
dance out of the riflemen's loins

become dessalines dessalines
la crête-a-pierrot
the spangle of death from the hot

of the trees
and christophe columbus climbs up to his mountain top
with the face of his horse in the faith of his shadow

he stumbles on priest on an ivory slave on a spaniard
the places of pain become pig snouts
the black becomes white becomes black becomes rain

falling to plunder the roof
of the world
toussaint is a zemi

he stares from the stone from the eye-
lids of flame
at his fate

New Year Letter

for mexican

The burnt out year
dies as the rocket
dies: cold sparks
to earth and ashes
to the earth, while
church bells mark
its passing

A brave new world
bursts as the rocket
bursts: hot sparks
to heaven and heaven
in the stars, while
church bells ring
the changes.
we too have known
this passing

We too have felt
the change. the cold
midnight unites and cleaves us.
hope dies, despair
like sparks is born,
bursts on our helpless
heaven in the brilliant air

And falls now
silently, dry
rain.
and falls now
soundlessly: the sky's
harsh waters will not flare
again

So softly now this moment fills
the darkness with its difference.
earth waits. trees touch
the dawn. despair, like sparks,
soon dies. so difference
dies. so darkness.
so let us face the new year
with clear eyes

3248